GRANDMA'S MEMORIES *for* MY GRANDCHILD

A Journal and Keepsake

WHITE STAR PUBLISHERS

PHOTO

A Story to Be Told...

A grandmother is a fundamental reference point during childhood, and a pivotal figure in the life of every child, offering loving attention, toys and immeasurable amounts of good advice and ideas, based on the wisdom gained throughout her long life. However, grandchildren often only a have very partial view of the grandmother figure. This book is therefore a way of getting to know her better, because every page can be used to collect the thoughts, stories, experiences and scenes of family life that your grandmother would like to share, opening the drawers of her memory so as to leave the new generations of her family with her life story and teachings for the future. The blank pages of this book, somewhere between a scrapbook and a diary, will gradually be filled with the stories of her life, immortalizing the past and thereby providing a precious guide for facing the future. It will therefore become an historical memoir and, at the same time, a testimony to the importance of one's roots.

Family Tree

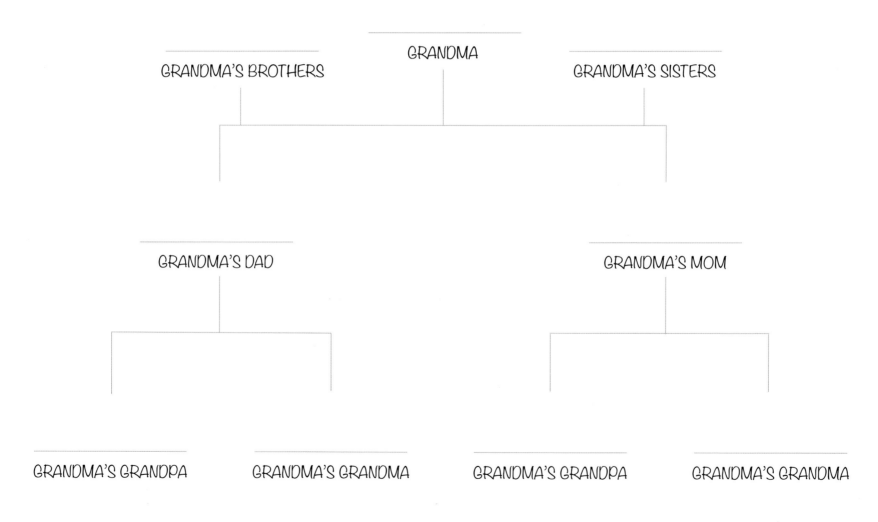

GRANDMA'S BROTHERS

GRANDMA

GRANDMA'S SISTERS

GRANDMA'S DAD

GRANDMA'S MOM

GRANDMA'S GRANDPA

GRANDMA'S GRANDMA

GRANDMA'S GRANDPA

GRANDMA'S GRANDMA

Our Family

PHOTO

PHOTO

Grandma, Tell Me Your Story...

When and where were you born?

_____

_____

_____

Tell me about your parents

_____

_____

_____

_____

_____

_____

_____

Tell me about your grandparents

_____

_____

_____

_____

_____

Tell me about your brothers and sisters

_____

_____

_____

_____

What was your house like?

What did you used to do on holidays?

_____

_____

_____

_____

_____

Do you remember a fairytale that you especially liked?

_____

_____

_____

_____

What was your favorite holiday?

Your Christmas

How did you celebrate Christmas?

_____

_____

_____

_____

Do you have any special memories?

_____

_____

_____

_____

_____

PHOTO

What are your fondest memories of your Mom?

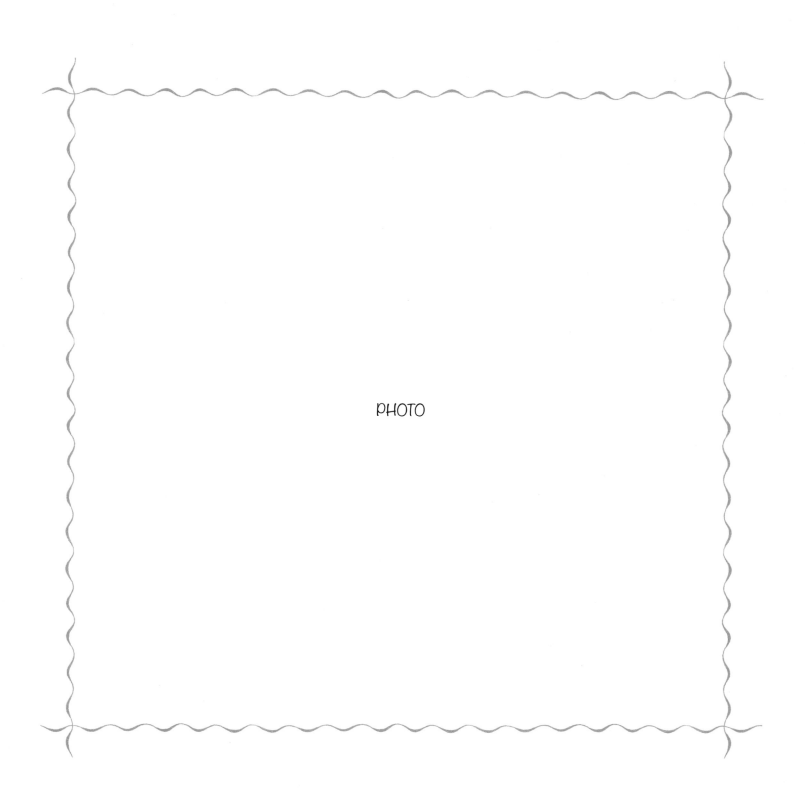

PHOTO

And of your Dad?

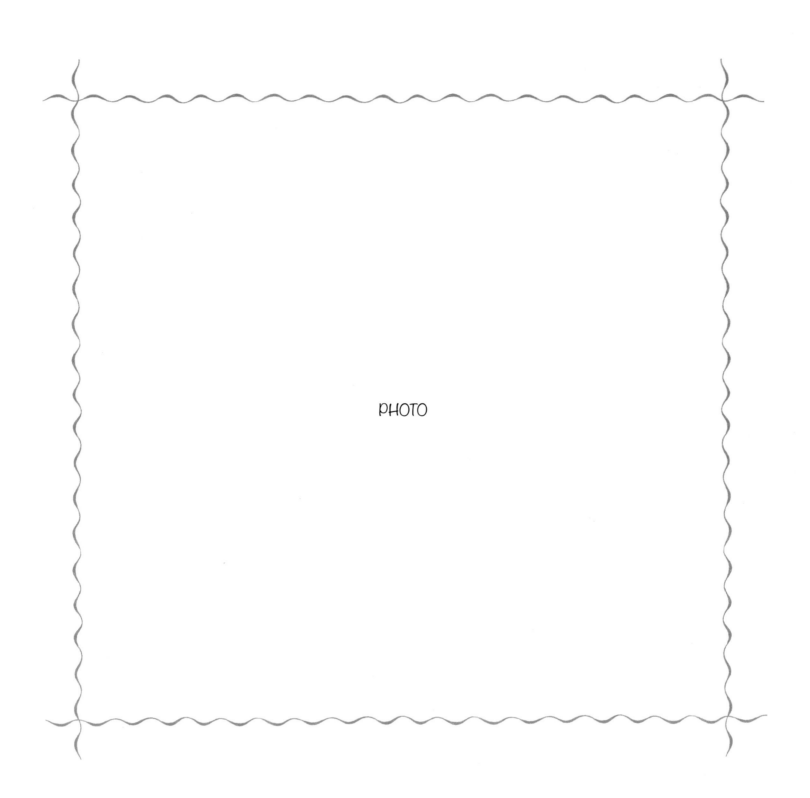

PHOTO

When You Were a Child...

What was your bedroom like?

Did you have a bedroom all to yourself?

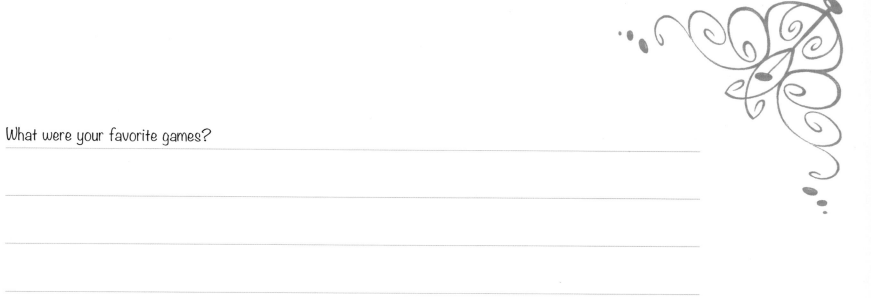

What were your favorite games?

_____

_____

_____

_____

_____

_____

Who did you go to when you needed help?

_____

_____

_____

_____

PHOTO

PHOTO

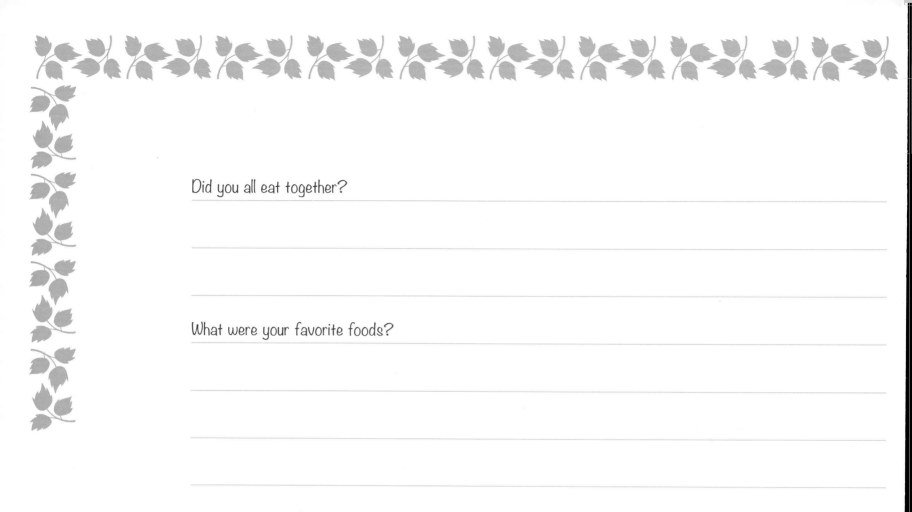

Did you all eat together?

What were your favorite foods?

What did you do after dinner?

Did you help your Mom do housework?

_____

_____

_____

_____

Did you have special house cleaning chores?

_____

_____

_____

_____

_____

_____

What did you do on Sunday?

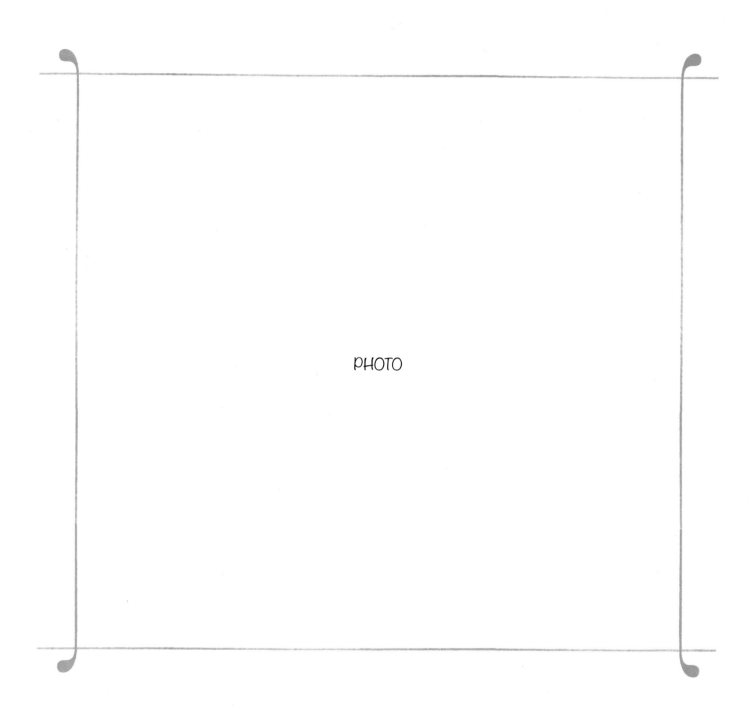

PHOTO

Who were your best friends?

_____

_____

_____

_____

What kind of games did you play?

_____

_____

_____

_____

_____

Did you play any sports?

PHOTO

PHOTO

PHOTO

At School

Do you remember your first day at school?

_____

_____

_____

_____

_____

_____

_____

_____

What was your school like?

_____

_____

_____

What was your teacher like?

_____

_____

_____

_____

How many classmates did you have and what were they like?

_____

_____

_____

_____

Who sat next to you?

_____

_____

PHOTO

What were your favorite subjects?

_____

_____

_____

_____

_____

Who took you to school?

_____

_____

_____

Which schools did you go to?

_____

_____

_____

What period of your school life did you like most and why?

_____

_____

_____

_____

_____

What were your dreams and aspirations after finishing school?

_____

_____

_____

_____

_____

PHOTO

PHOTO

How did you spend your time during summer vacation?

PHOTO

Your Job

What was your first job after school? How old were you?

Did you change jobs often? Tell me about it!

When You Met Grandpa...

When and where did you meet grandpa?

_____

_____

_____

_____

_____

_____

_____

How old were you?

_____

_____

_____

What struck you about him?

_____

_____

_____

_____

_____

_____

_____

_____

What was it about him that made him special?

When did you introduce him to your friends?

What did they say?

What did you like doing together?

What did you talk about?

Did you have lots of friends?

When and how did he ask you to marry him?

PHOTO

PHOTO

Your Wedding

When did you get married?

_____

_____

Tell me about your wedding

_____

_____

_____

_____

_____

_____

_____

_____

PHOTO

PHOTO

Where did you get married?

What was grandpa wearing?

Were you excited?

Who was there? What was the reception like?

PHOTO

PHOTO

Your Honeymoon

Where did you go on your honeymoon? What are your favorite memories?

PHOTO

PHOTO

The Start of a New Life...

Where did you go to live?

_____

_____

_____

What was your house like?

_____

_____

_____

_____

_____

_____

_____

When did you find out that you were going to be a mom?

_____

_____

_____

How did Grandpa react when you told him?

_____

_____

_____

_____

How did your life together change?

_____

_____

_____

_____

_____

What was Dad/Mom like when he/she was a child?

Who did he/she look like?

Photos of Dad/Mom when he/she was little

PHOTO

Tell me something else about Dad/Mom

_____

_____

_____

_____

_____

_____

Was he/she obedient?

_____

_____

_____

_____

How did he/she get to school?

_____

_____

_____

_____

_____

Did he/she ever get into huge trouble?

_____

_____

_____

_____

_____

_____

What are the happiest memories of your marriage?

_____

_____

_____

_____

_____

What are the saddest memories?

_____

_____

_____

_____

_____

Did you celebrate holidays with your family?

_____

_____

_____

Tell me about your vacations

_____

_____

_____

_____

_____

_____

_____

_____

PHOTO

PHOTO

...and Then I Arrived!

How did you feel about becoming a grandma?

What did you think when you saw me for the first time?

How did your life change?

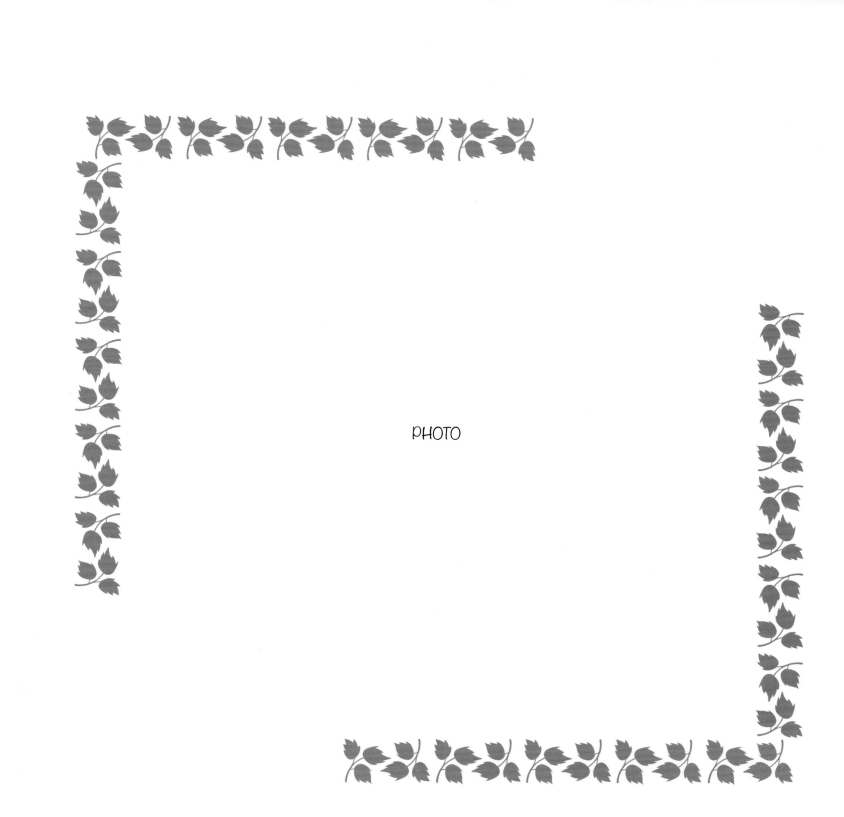

PHOTO

Which historical events do you remember during your lifetime?

Are you nostalgic about the olden days?

What do you think about the world today?

Do you have any regrets?

_____

_____

_____

_____

_____

Would you change anything about your life?

_____

_____

_____

_____

_____

What message would you like to leave for your family?

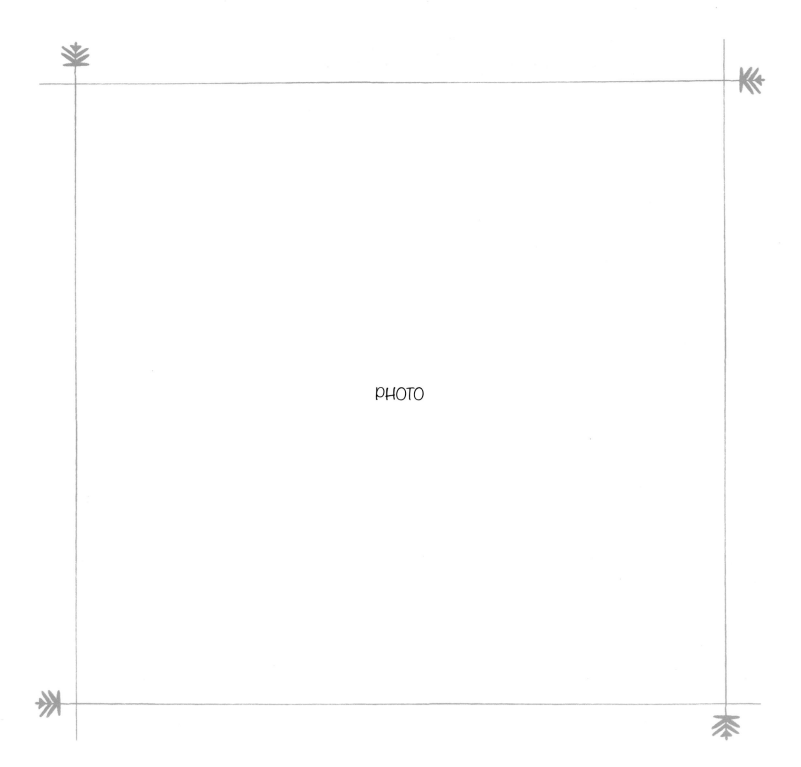

PHOTO

The Story Continues...

Illustrations

Francesca Rossi

Graphic Layout

Paola Piacco

WS WHITE STAR PUBLISHERS

WS White Star Publishers® is a registered trademark
property of White Star s.r.l.

© 2019 White Star s.r.l.
Piazzale Luigi Cadorna, 6 - 20123 Milan, Italy
www.whitestar.it

Translation and Editing: TperTradurre s.r.l.

ISBN 978-88-544-1517-1
1 2 3 4 5 6   23 22 21 20 19

Printed in China